Floods

Catherine Chambers

Heinemann
LIBRARY

www.heinemann.co.uk
Visit our website to find out more information about Heinemann Library books.

To order:
☎ Phone 44 (0) 1865 888066
📄 Send a fax to 44 (0) 1865 314091
💻 Visit the Heinemann Bookshop at www.heinemann.co.uk to browse our catalogue
and order online.

First published in Great Britain by Heinemann Library, Halley Court, Jordan Hill, Oxford OX2 8EJ
a division of Reed Educational and Professional Publishing Ltd. Heinemann is a registered trademark of
Reed Educational & Professional Publishing Ltd.

OXFORD MELBOURNE AUCKLAND JOHANNESBURG BLANTYRE
GABORONE IBADAN PORTSMOUTH (NH) USA CHICAGO

Designed by Celia Floyd
Originated by Dot Gradations
Printed by Wing King Tong, in Hong Kong

04 03 02 01 00
10 9 8 7 6 5 4 3 2 1

ISBN 0 431 09604 X

British Library Cataloguing in Publication Data

Chambers, Catherine
  Floods. – (Disasters in Nature)
  1. Floods – Juvenile literature
  I. Title
  551.5'89

Acknowledgements

The Publishers would like to thank the following for permission to reproduce photographs:

Bruce Coleman Collection: pg.40; *Environmental Images*: Paul Glendell pg.22; *Environmental Picture
Library*: C Jones pg.34. Rob Visser pg.37; *FLPA*: David Warren pg.35, Derek Hall, pg.6, G Marcoaldi/Panda
pg.25, John Bastable pg.15, W Broadhurst pg.33; *Image Bank*: Thomas Schmitt pg.39; *Katz Pictures*:
Silva/Agenzia Contrasto pg.29; *NHPA*: David Middleton pg.38; *Oxford Scientific Films*: Daniel J Cox pg.43,
Lon E Lauber pg.32; *Panos*: Jim Holmes pg.9, Trygre Bølstad pg.7, Betty Press pg.11, pg.26; *Photri*: H
Hungerford pg.21; *Popperfoto*: Reuters pg.45; *Science Photo Library*: John Mead pg.27, NASA pg.17; *Tony
Stone*: Graeme Norways pg.41, Hugh Sitton pg.5, Martin Puddy pg.13, Warren Jacobs pg.30.

Cover photograph reproduced with permission of Robert Harding Picture Library.

Our thanks to Mandy Barker for her comments in the preparation of this book.

Every effort has been made to contact copyright holders of any material reproduced in this book. Any
omissions will be rectified in subsequent printings if notice is given to the Publisher.

Any words appearing in the text in bold, **like this**, are explained in the Glossary.

Contents

Introduction

What is a flood?

A flood is a swelling, surging body of water rising well above its normal highest level, bursting the banks of river channels, canals, lakes, the sea coast and dams and spilling over the land. Sometimes floodwaters creep up slowly but at other times sudden **flash floods** seem to appear from nowhere.

Some floods are annual events. People expect and prepare for them. Sometimes they can turn into a catastrophe. Then, water, mud and debris kill or displace people and animals. Buildings are destroyed and plants are suffocated. Floodwater can be a very destructive force, so recovery from a serious flood disaster can take a long time for both the human and the natural world.

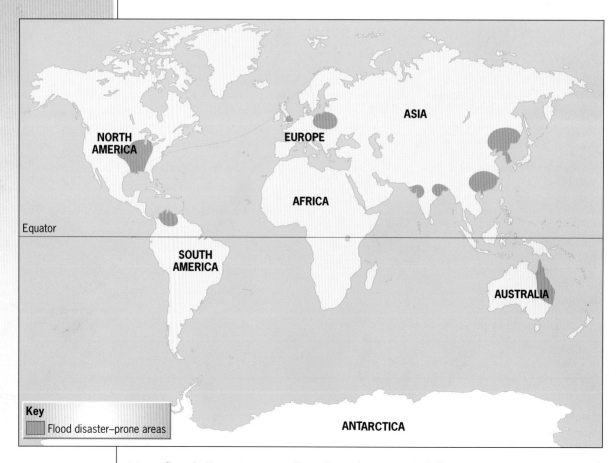

Most flood disaster zones lie where heavy rainfall is concentrated in just a few days, or even hours.

Where in the world?

Flood disaster occurs along some of the world's greatest **floodplains**, river valleys and **deltas** – along the Hwang He and Yangtze in China, the grand rivers Brahmaputra and Ganges in Bangladesh and the mighty Mississippi and Missouri in the United States. They also occur in places where torrential rainfall from **cyclones inundates** the land, from the west coast of Australia to the shores of northern Europe. The worst flood hazard areas are shown in the map opposite.

Flood in our hands and on our minds

The number of flood disasters seems to have increased in recent years. Is this because we hear more about them in the media, or is it due to changes in the world's climate – or even because more people now live in the areas that are at risk? Some scientists believe that **global warming** and the **El Niño** effect are to blame. Are these just part of the natural cycle of the world's climate – or are we contributing to the problem? Scientists do agree that humans have contributed to flood disaster by **deforestation**, **soil erosion** and altering the course of river channels.

When floods are expected or managed, farmers can prepare their land and plant crops such as rice in flooded fields.

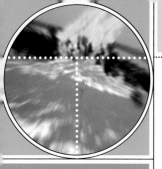

Bangladesh – a waterworld

It is almost impossible to imagine your whole world – everything as far as the eye can see – covered in water. This is what people in a huge area of Bangladesh experience every year.

Monsoon rains

During the summer **monsoon** rains, when warm, wet winds blow northward onto the coast, floods occur in many parts of Bangladesh. It is situated on a lowlying **floodplain**, where the great Meghna, Brahmaputra and Ganges rivers wind slowly towards the sea. Normal floods are called **borsha**, and cover 20–30 per cent of Bangladesh. Heavier floods bringing disaster to the area are called **bonna**. Borsha floods bring fertility to the soil and an opportunity to farm and fish. The floodwaters also flush out salts from the soil. These salts often occur in waterlogged areas and can make the land infertile if they are not washed away.

Three main crops of rice are grown in Bangladesh at different times over the year. Usually at least one rice crop is successful, even if there is heavy flooding.

The floods of 1988

One of the most devastating floods in recent times occurred in 1988 when nearly 60 per cent of the land was submerged. Instead of flooding at separate times, usually over a four-month period, the Meghna, Brahmaputra and Ganges all burst their banks within two weeks.

Floods normally occur here because torrential monsoon rains swell the rivers from May to September. In 1988, there was just too much rain in a short space of time running off the Himalaya mountain range. Rivers burst their banks overnight and water gushed onto 122 000 square kilometres (about 47 000 square miles) of land in just 24 hours – that's about two-thirds of the country.

Many houses were damaged or completely lost in the severe floods of 1988 in Bangladesh.

The loss of life and damage were colossal: 2379 people died, either through drowning or disease spread by the floodwater. There were no clean water supplies, as water became **contaminated** with sewage. Over half a million livestock animals drowned, two million tonnes of rice were destroyed, over seven million homes were flattened and hundreds of kilometres of roads, railways and bridges were damaged.

7

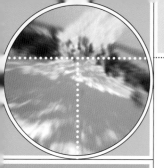

After the disaster

Watching and warning

After the 1987 and 1988 floods, Bangladesh has put in place a complex flood protection system. It monitors a wide range of factors including changes in snow density in the Himalaya mountain range, any change in a river's course and measures water **discharge** and the movement of **sediment**. From these and many other statistics, **hazard maps** can be drawn up to highlight the danger zones.

Together, the measures can predict floods at least two weeks in advance – in theory! The situation in Bangladesh is so complicated, and flood factors so sudden, that disaster is not always predictable.

A grand plan?

The World Bank has prepared and is co-ordinating a Flood Action Plan in Bangladesh. The idea is to construct channels called dykes along the banks of the Meghna and Brahmaputra rivers. This is so that floodwaters have an outlet and will not bring flood disaster. There is widespread local and international opposition to this plan, which would take 20 years to complete at a cost of £6.25 billion (US$10 billion), which neither aid donors nor a poor country such as Bangladesh can afford. It is thought that the system will not offer foolproof protection against flood disaster and will stop the benefits brought by the normal **borsha** floods.

Some of the flooding is caused by heavy rainfall on the land itself, not just by burst river banks. For this reason alone, the flood plan will not succeed.

Other ways of preventing flood disaster are being considered but they are all expensive. Flood prediction, preparation and education are already in hand. These are cheaper ways to save lives.

The flood waters bring benefits too – fishing brings in extra food.

Positive and negative

The advantages of floodwaters in Bangladesh have encouraged millions of people to live on the **floodplain**, putting up homes on stilts embedded in clay embankments. Obviously, all these buildings, and schools and hospitals constructed in the same way, are vulnerable to flood disaster. So are any roads and railways linking settlements in these areas.

With hardly any industry, people have very little choice but to live in these hazardous farming areas. The floodwaters from the Himalaya mountain range bring not only water but also important **nitrate** and **phosphate** chemicals to the soils. Farmers use only traditional tools and farming methods, yet bumper harvests are common in such fertile lands. It is easy to see why millions of people live on the floodplains of Bangladesh, but it is also easy to see that when flood disaster comes, it destroys most economic activity.

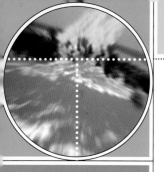

Hitting the headlines

A smaller world

The flood disaster of 1988 certainly hit the headlines. It led to an international effort to provide better flood prevention, control and prediction systems. Bangladesh's most recent flood disaster occurred in 1998 and this, too, was widely reported by news networks throughout the world. Other major catastrophes affected the area in 1988, 1987, 1974, 1955 and 1954. It is difficult to say whether flood disasters are occurring more frequently or whether they are now just more accurately measured and more heavily reported in the media.

Through satellite communications and the Internet, news of a disaster can reach most parts of the developed world within minutes. It probably travels faster in the United States than in any other part of the world. As we shall see on page 27, the US uses a flood warning system called **ALERT** to warn people of a potential disaster. Flood-measuring instruments are linked to warning systems and television networks. Once news media know of a looming disaster, they can then transmit the information not only to the locally affected communities, but all over the world.

Flood fact

- During the floods that washed across northern Italy in November 1966, 800 communities were affected, 112 people were killed and 50 000 farm animals were drowned, but it was the beautiful city of Florence that attracted worldwide media attention. This was because mud and flood debris destroyed many priceless treasures including books, paintings, sculptures and architecture.

Rich and poor

In poorer nations where there is less money for looking after communication networks such as roads and railways, there is still often a time lag of several hours or even days between the disaster taking place and the news reaching the rest of the world. Added to this, richer nations often do not use their vast media resources to report stories in poor, remote parts of the world. When they do, they often have to rely on interpreters and aid agencies to pull together a story, which can lead to distortion of the facts.

Honduras, like other poorer nations, suffers terrible economic problems in the wake of a flood disaster. This banana crop was destroyed by Hurricane Mitch.

Hidden floods

Flooding occurs in the Brazilian rainforest every year and its effect on the natural world is quite dramatic but we do not see it reported in the media. This is mostly because this annual flooding rarely causes human disaster, as it is slow-rising, expected and well-managed. The people who live there build homes and animal shelters suited to the conditions.

Flood disasters are often neglected because other news stories dominate the headlines. In parts of Europe in the 1990s, the war in the Balkan countries of the former Yugoslavia was often given top priority.

11

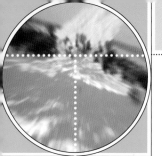

What brings the rain?

Rain is part of the **water cycle**. This term describes the way in which the Earth's supply of water is recycled all the time in different forms. Sometimes it is held in the air as invisible **water vapour** or as tiny droplets in clouds, sometimes it falls as rain, snow, sleet or hail. But most of it lies in massive oceans, seas and lakes, or it is frozen in ice sheets and glaciers. There is always the same amount of water on the Earth, even if we cannot actually see some of it. But the water cycle is a very fast global system. This makes it almost impossible to predict accurately.

Sun, wind and rain

When the Sun shines and the wind blows over the oceans and great lakes, water **evaporates** from the surface. If the air above the water is warm it holds a lot of vapour, as warm air can hold more moisture than cold air. Warm air is also less dense than cold air. This means that its molecules are spaced further apart, which makes the warm air lighter. The warm, moist air rises, and the vapour **condenses** into tiny droplets which form clouds.

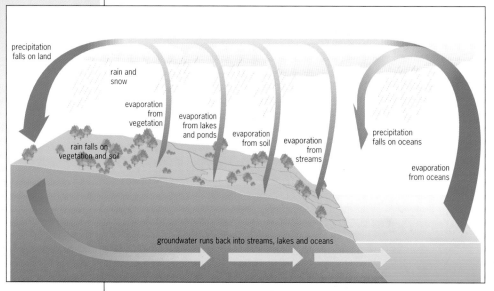

precipitation falls on land

rain and snow

evaporation from vegetation

evaporation from lakes and ponds

evaporation from soil

evaporation from streams

precipitation falls on oceans

evaporation from oceans

rain falls on vegetation and soil

groundwater runs back into streams, lakes and oceans

The amount of water that evaporates and turns into rain depends a lot on how much heat from the Sun reaches the Earth.

As cloud gets higher, it reaches the much colder air in the Earth's atmosphere. The water vapour and tiny droplets inside the cloud cool and condense into larger water droplets. The droplets become too heavy to stay in the high clouds, so they fall to the ground as rain. Some rain falls on the oceans, but a lot falls on land. Clouds rise up high hill and mountain slopes, shedding rain before they reach the other side. The drops fall down the slope, gathering in tiny streams. The streams flow into rivers, and the rivers into seas, and the cycle begins all over again.

Collecting water

Each river runs through a **catchment area**, from which all surface and underground water finds its way to that river. Each catchment area lies in its own river basin, which is divided from its neighbouring basin by higher ground known as a **watershed**. A river is fed not only by the streams that run into it but also by the water that seeps through the soil. Later on we shall see how humans have changed the natural flow of rivers and absorption of water into the ground by **deforestation**. It makes flood disaster more likely by causing greater **run-off**, when water runs freely down a slope. It also means that more soil is washed away and down into rivers where it can block and flood the channel.

'Monsoon' conjures up images of torrential rain in hot, steamy climates but, in fact, the word comes from the Arabic word for season.

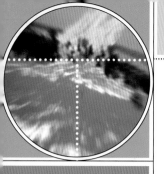

Hurricanes and storm surges

A **hurricane** is a fierce whirling wind that blows in an inward spiral from an area of **high pressure** to an area of **low pressure**. It is at its strongest in warm, tropical and subtropical areas. A hurricane is known also as a tropical **cyclone** or a **typhoon**, depending on where it occurs. Hurricanes not only bring raging winds – they also form savage **storm surges** – huge waves that cover the coast and cause flood disaster.

How do hurricanes happen?

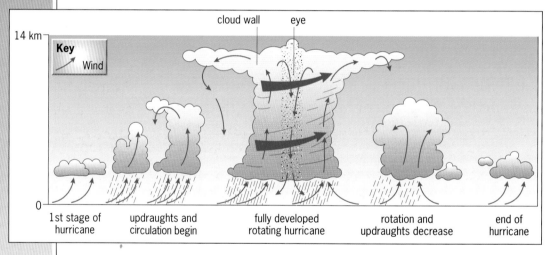

As the hurricane approaches land, it picks up more moisture, and its swirling winds blow ever faster. At the same time, the whole hurricane moves forwards faster until it runs out of 'fuel' and dies down over the land.

It is thought that hurricanes form as masses of warm, very moist air rise, reducing pressure over the oceans. Areas of very low air pressure grow as the warm air rises in a whirling, upward spiral. Cooler air from an area of high pressure rushes into the space it has created. As the warm air goes up, it cools and the moisture in the air **condenses**, forming banks of very

heavy, lowlying raincloud. The formation of cloud also releases heat into the air, which fuels the whirling hurricane even more. The upward-turning spiral and rushing winds get faster and faster as they approach land. Once the hurricane moves over the land, there is no more warm moisture to pick up – the fuel runs out. The hurricane slowly dies but the damage on the coast has already been done.

Disaster on the coast

Hurricane storm surges are created by low pressure and whirling winds sucking up the sea, so that a huge wall of water rises and drives towards the shore. Some waves can reach a height of 8 metres (30 feet) causing severe coastal flooding. This is made worse by a rise in sea level of up to 50 centimetres (20 inches), caused again by low pressure over the sea, drawing the water upward. Torrential rain and a high tide cause further havoc. It is estimated that 90 per cent of all deaths along a flooded coast are caused by drowning.

The polder lands in the Netherlands are very lowlying, flat areas of farmland which have been reclaimed from the sea. In February 1953, a huge storm surge flooded the polders, killing nearly 2000 people, and destroying almost half a million buildings.

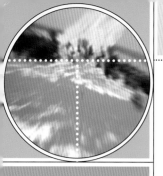

Global warming

The world's climate is getting warmer and although scientists cannot agree whether **global warming** causes more flood disaster or more drought, it does seem that we have suffered greater extremes of wetness and dryness in the last 20 years. It takes a difference of only 1–2° Celsius (about 2–4° Fahrenheit) to change the Earth's climate and weather patterns quite dramatically. Scientists think that in 30 years' time temperatures all over the world will have risen by 1° Celsius (about 2° Fahrenheit). This rise is especially important in coastal areas where there is risk of floods. If the temperature rises, winds passing over the oceans will **evaporate** more water into the air, so more will fall as rain on land.

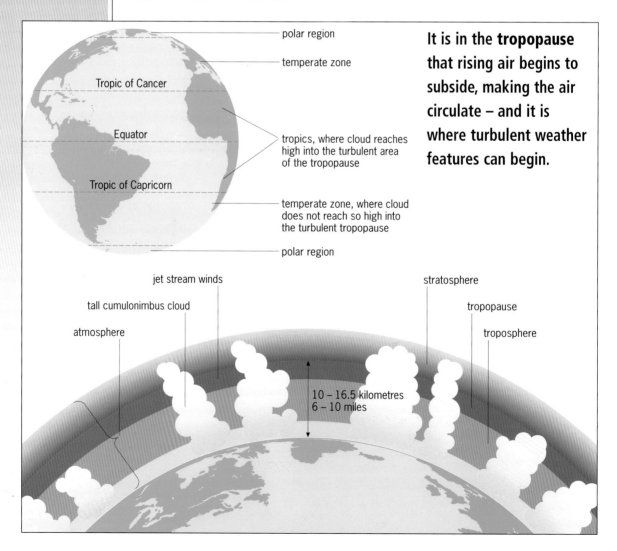

polar region

temperate zone

Tropic of Cancer

Equator

Tropic of Capricorn

tropics, where cloud reaches high into the turbulent area of the tropopause

temperate zone, where cloud does not reach so high into the turbulent tropopause

polar region

It is in the **tropopause** that rising air begins to subside, making the air circulate – and it is where turbulent weather features can begin.

jet stream winds

tall cumulonimbus cloud

atmosphere

stratosphere

tropopause

troposphere

10 – 16.5 kilometres
6 – 10 miles

Under glass

Many people believe that global warming is caused, at least partly, by the **greenhouse effect**. This is caused by certain gases, particularly carbon dioxide, rising into the atmosphere. Heat from the Sun is absorbed by the Earth and some is reflected and **radiated** back. These gases form a layer which acts like a huge mirror, reflecting this radiated heat back down to Earth and warming the sea and the land.

About 80 per cent of the **carbon gases** are produced when **fossil fuels** such as coal and oil are burned in power stations, factories and homes. But the greenhouse effect and global warming are not thought to be acting on their own to cause climatic change.

A hole in the sky

Earth is surrounded by layers of gases known as the atmosphere. This stops the full strength of the Sun's energy from reaching the Earth, and filters harmful **ultra-violet rays**. One of the most effective protective gases is **ozone**, which forms a layer in the **stratosphere**, 10–50 kilometres (about 6–30 miles) above the surface of the Earth. In recent years the ozone layer has become thinner, especially over Antarctica, and one of the effects of this is increased radiation from the Sun.

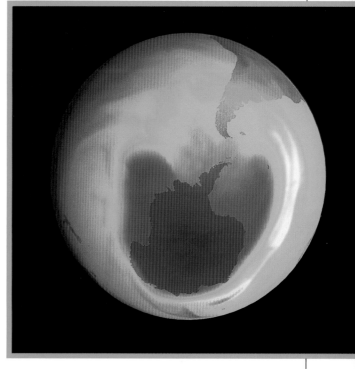

This satellite picture shows the size and shape of the ozone hole over Antarctica (the dark blue land) in October 1999. The ozone hole is shown by the darkest shades of blue.

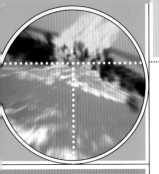

The effects of El Niño

In recent years **El Niño** has been the most talked-about cause of freak natural disasters all over the world. This phenomenon can bring torrential rain and heavy flooding, violent **hurricanes** and terrifying tornadoes.

The phenomenon was first noticed by anchovy fishermen off the coast of Peru. Every few years the cold coastal waters and the air above them warmed up and brought welcome rain to the dry shores of Peru around Christmas time. Over the years, this mild, welcome climatic variation has turned into a dreaded disaster. El Niño has brought violent storms, flooding the coast, damaging homes and breaking bridges. Sometimes El Niño is followed by **La Niña**, a dramatic and often treacherous reversal of winds and ocean currents.

These maps shows the dramatic effects of El Niño and its opposite, La Niña. Scientists are still studying the effects of ocean currents on El Niño and La Niña winds.

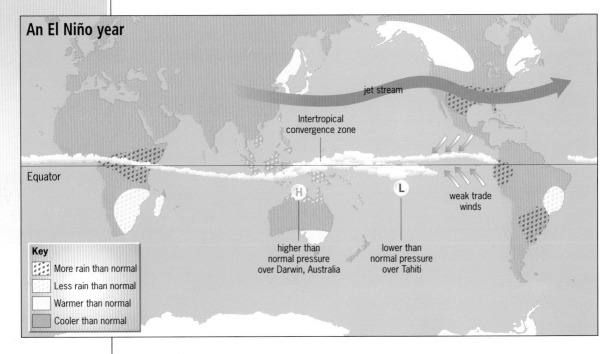

An El Niño year

jet stream

Intertropical convergence zone

Equator

H — higher than normal pressure over Darwin, Australia

L — lower than normal pressure over Tahiti

weak trade winds

Key

More rain than normal
Less rain than normal
Warmer than normal
Cooler than normal

The power of El Niño

El Niño is a very complicated climatic feature, affecting most of the globe. In the Pacific Ocean, it begins with a change in the temperature of the sea. This leads to a sudden reversal of the prevailing winds – the winds that blow in a predictable direction all year round. Scientists believe that a similar phenomenon takes place above the Atlantic Ocean. These dramatic changes in the atmosphere do not act on their own. It is believed that changes in the oceans' powerful currents affect the weather patterns above.

El Niños of the past

We can find out a lot about El Niños of the past by studying tree rings (see page 43), soil **sediments** at the bottom of the ocean, ice cores from thick ice at the poles, and coral reefs. When this information is compared with written and spoken accounts of past climatic disasters, the results are amazing, linking El Niños with disasters such as the potato blight and the famine which followed in Ireland in the 1840s.

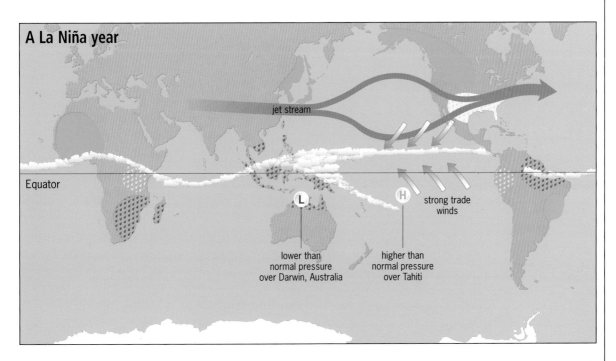

A La Niña year

jet stream

Equator

L — lower than normal pressure over Darwin, Australia

H — higher than normal pressure over Tahiti

strong trade winds

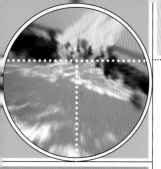

Rising rivers

Why does the river flood?

Most flooding along the course of a river occurs at its flattest part, called the **floodplain**. This forms once the river has left the mountains and is winding across flat land on its way to the sea. Here, the river's channel is often shallow, containing thick layers of **silt** that has been washed down from the upper reaches of the river. This means that any floodwaters cannot flow fast and freely down the river, and so they spill out over the banks onto the floodplain.

Flood facts

All flooding occurs when the balance between the following elements (the 'water balance') is disturbed – when there is so much water on the land that it cannot be soaked up by the rock and soil, carried away by rivers or **evaporated** into the air.

- **precipitation** – rain, sleet, hail, snow or mist

- **evaporation** – when water and moisture in the soil is heated and changes into **water vapour**, which is a gas

- **evapotranspiration** – the loss of water by evaporation, and by transpiration through plant leaves

- **run-off** – water flowing freely downhill into a river or stream

- storage – the amount of water that **percolates** (seeps) down into the ground or saturates the soil

- **throughflow** – the amount of water that runs through the ground and into a stream, river or lake

Along the marshy course of the Mississippi in the US canals, **levees** (higher river banks) and dykes (drainage ditches) have been built. This has squeezed parts of the river's course into an unnatural, deep channel, making a greater volume of water run faster onto areas that are still flat and unaltered. Flooding here is made worse. This photo shows what happened when the Mississippi broke out of its channel in Illinois in July 1993. ⟶

The ways of the river

The shape of the river channel, the slope of the land around it and the thickness of the silt on the river bed affect the river's **discharge** – the amount of water that passes a certain point at a particular time. The ability of the surrounding land to soak up rainwater also affects discharge. Heavy rainfall on **impermeable** soils, like fine clay, that do not soak up water easily, causes run-off. This is water that streams across the surface of the land and drains straight into the river, quickly raising water levels.

The more a river rages upstream, the more deposits are eroded and brought down onto the floodplain. Over many years, layers of silt build up into banks. The river winds around the banks and these winding curves, called **meanders**, slow the river, making flooding even more likely. Straightening the river's course only creates worse problems downstream – water rushes too quickly onto the lower floodplain or into the river **estuary**. Near the sea, tidal saltmarshes are flood hotspots too.

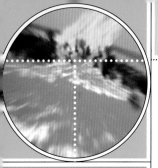

The power of the waves

Flooding at the coast occurs mainly around **estuaries**, where the river fans out and flows into the sea. Unfortunately, there are often large settlements around these areas. Flood disaster here is often caused by a deadly combination of three freak natural conditions. Torrential rainfall swells the rivers, causing water to rush down onto the coastal **floodplain**. High tide is higher than usual, so waves push up the estuary, meeting the flooded river waters coming the other way. Added to this, a **storm surge** creates a massive wave which smothers the coast.

This picture shows another kind of water surge, called a **tidal bore**, on the Severn estuary in Britain. Surfers take advantage of a high bulge of seawater, made by an extra-high tide, that rolls up an estuary and pushes the river waters backwards forming a heavy wall of water.

Creating waves

Normally, a beach is a natural coastal defence system, stopping waves from eating too quickly into land and preventing coastal flooding. Beaches are made of loose material – sand, shingle and pebbles – so waves can build them into shapes. Sand ripples and shingle ridges all soften the impact of waves, making them less destructive. When storm waves do batter cliffs and erode them, the material is deposited along the base of the cliff. It makes a platform called a storm beach, which tends to protect the cliff from further erosion – at least for a while.

Wave action usually forms a cycle of building and flattening, which evens out the force of water against the rigid land. This cycle only operates in normal conditions. Storm surges make sudden attacks on cliffs, then they flood beaches, pushing sand and shingle into dunes. The dunes swallow up more land, covering coastal paths and roads. The natural balance of wave action and beach-building is disturbed by a single sudden freak condition and the system has to rebuild its natural cycle.

Ocean tides

High tides and low tides are created mainly by the Moon's gravity and, to a lesser extent, the Sun's, pulling the seas from one side of the world to the other. The Moon attracts the water as it moves around the Earth, creating bulges, or high tides. Every fourteen days, the Moon and the Sun are set in a straight line and pull together on the Earth. This makes higher high tides, called **spring tides**. These can cause flooding, especially if they are accompanied by high winds.

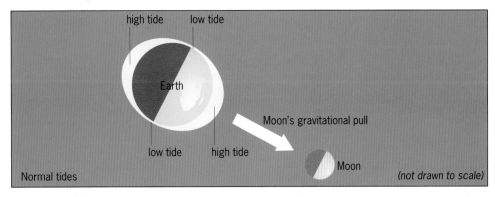

The positions of the Moon and Sun are what control the tides.

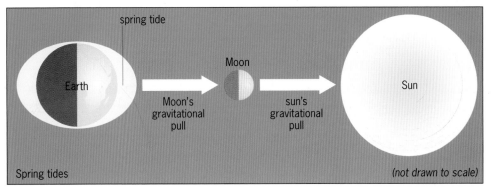

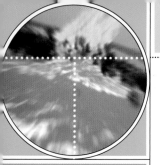

Measuring and predicting

Flood hydrographs

Flooding can occur quickly and heavily, or it can creep up slowly but take a long time to go down. Clearly, it is important to know the amount and type of flooding that can occur along a particular stretch of a river. One of the most valuable tools used to find out what happens when rain falls on a flood hazard zone is the storm (or flood) **hydrograph**.

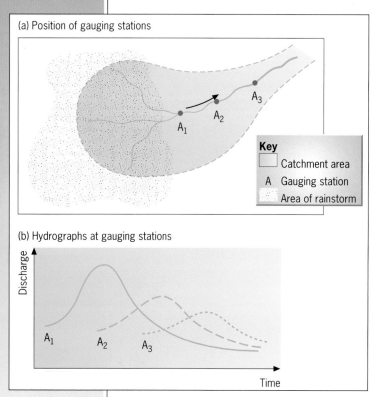

(a) Position of gauging stations

A_1 A_2 A_3

Key
- Catchment area
- A Gauging station
- Area of rainstorm

(b) Hydrographs at gauging stations

Discharge

A_1 A_2 A_3

Time

The flood hydrograph shows how quickly and how high waters are rising, and when they reach their peak **discharge**.

A storm hydrograph placed at gauging stations along a river (a) measures the amount of water that passes a certain point in a river, after rainfall. It varies according to how much rain falls in and around the river, how much water is **evaporated**, and the amount of water stored in the channel. The graph (b) shows what happens to a stream when rain falls. One of the most important measurements is the time it takes for all the rainfall to reach the channel. This is called the **lag-time**. This does not just include the rain falling directly onto the channel, but all the water that runs or soaks into it as well. Knowing lag-time is crucial for predicting flood disaster.

Mudslides are caused when soil lying on a slope is so wet that it is too heavy to stick to the underlying rock or soil. Gravity pulls the mud downwards, carrying everything on top of it. In Campania in Italy, in May 1998, torrential rain caused these massive mudslides.

What affects the lag-time?

Lag-time is affected by rock and soil type. If ground is **impermeable**, water will run off into the channel quite quickly, raising water levels with great speed. If it is **permeable**, water will soak in and take longer to reach the channel. The effects of soil and rock on flooding depend on the amount and type of **precipitation** that occurs. In long periods of heavy rainfall, even permeable soils can get **saturated** so that water runs off very fast.

Lag-time and us

Human activity can affect lag-time as much as nature. Vegetation such as trees and bushes slows down precipitation reaching the soil, so much less water flows as **run-off** or reaches the channel by soaking into the ground. When we cut down trees and clear away bushes, precipitation can fall directly onto the ground. Then more water reaches the channel and it gets there faster. Growing cities – urbanization – also make flooding more likely, as the pressure of buildings on the land raises the water table.

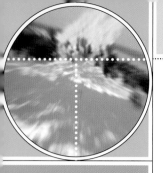

Flood alert!

Modern technology helps us to predict the length and intensity of rainstorms and of flooding in a particular place. In most countries, this information is monitored by national weather services which issue flood warnings when conditions are severe. This is especially important when large regions are affected, as it takes a lot of time and organization to **evacuate** so many people. National meteorological offices have direct communication with all emergency services and to television and radio networks. Radio, television, the police and other emergency services – and now the Internet – are all used to warn people about flooding.

But flooding often occurs at a very local level, around small isolated towns and villages. In these places, conditions leading to flooding are not big enough to be monitored by a national weather service, so local prediction and warning systems are put into place.

In the United States, about £3.40 (US$5.5) is spent per person, every year on flood repair. That's a staggering £940 million pounds (US$1.5 billion)! But in many poorer, developing countries, like Honduras, shown in this photograph, flood warnings are not organized on a national scale and come too late to evacuate people. Flood disaster can wreck their fragile economy.

Slow floods and flash floods

It is much easier to give successful flood warnings where water usually rises very slowly. Along the Mississippi, for example, several stages of flood alert can often be issued as much as a week in advance. This gives people a lot of time to prepare. But **flash floods** are another matter and an immediate emergency warning needs to be given.

In the United States flash floods are quite common. They often occur in **hurricane** zones, where rainfall can be very intense. In these and other flash flood areas, automatic sensors measure streamflow, and raingauges measure **precipitation**. Radio transmitters relay the measurements to a computer. This puts all the data together and issues a warning if necessary. The system is known as **ALERT** (Automated Local Evaluation in Real Time).

In parts of the United States, scientists measure any movement of the rocks around dams especially in earthquake zones. An earthquake could break the dam causing huge floods. This is Shasta Dam in California.

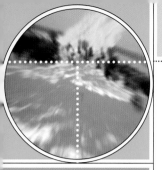

Why live in danger?

People live in flood hotspots sometimes by choice – flood hazard zones are often very beautiful. Tourists flock to them, too. However, most people who live in floods zones live there because they have to. This is where they make their living.

Living on the floodplain

It is no accident that great civilizations developed along **floodplains**. The ancient Egyptians along the Nile and the Sumerians between the Tigris and Euphrates are just two examples. It was in these regions that natural flooding enabled huge areas of land to be cultivated. This encouraged people from other areas to make their homes on the floodplains – and the increasing population created a need for political and economic organization, law and order, and culture such as literature, art and music.

In countries such as Bangladesh, Vietnam and China, the floodplain provides farmland and fisheries. The river is actually home, too, where floating and raised houses can be constructed. Its waterways are the main means of transport.

Where the river meets the sea

Farming and fishing are not the only activities along floodplains. Great industrial cities have emerged along the river banks. Water is an important factor in deciding where to locate industry. Chemical, paper, steel and textile industries all use a lot of water in the manufacturing process and in disposing of waste. Some of the world's heaviest industrial areas lie along floodplains of the major rivers such as the Danube, Rhone, Mississippi, Rhine, Volga, Seine – and the Mersey in Britain, often considered the cradle of European industrialization.

Added to this, floodplains provide a flat surface on which to build homes, factories, road and rail networks and airports. Most governments with huge flood-risk areas have created **hazard maps** so that developers can avoid building on the most dangerous parts, but these are largely ignored.

The Italian city of Venice grew up as a successful trading port, dealing in silks and spices from the Far East. The world's first banking system was established in the city, and it became a large manufacturing centre famous for its glass, glass beads, mirrors, tapestries and textiles. Venice lies between the Po and Piave rivers, on the Adriatic Sea – a perfect position for trading with many parts of the world. It is built on piles set on 170 low, barrier islands between the two rivers. Shipbuilding and heavy industry now lie on the city's outskirts.

Over three-quarters of Venice is at sea level and is flooded by storms every winter. Raised walkways helped people to get around in these floods in 1996.

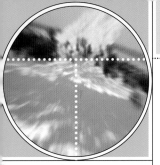

Controlling the floods

Floodwaters are one of the most destructive forces on Earth. So how can they be controlled? Many types of structural flood protection methods have been put into place all over the world for thousands of years.

Learning from the past

One of the simplest and oldest ways of controlling flooding is terracing, used right round the world from China in the Far East, through Peru in South America, to Ethiopia in the Horn of Africa. Terraces are platforms cut into the hillside, with stone or earth walls around the edges. Crops are grown inside the walls, which collect rainwater to **irrigate** the land. The terraces also help to stop **run-off** in a heavy rainstorm.

Part of the Flood Action Plan for Bangladesh includes creating basins by the riverbanks so that floodwaters flow into them rather than **inundate** the **floodplain**. This is a very old idea, too. Ancient Egyptians dug basin-shaped fields along the Nile floodplain. These were filled by the annual floodwaters, which gradually drained away, leaving rich soil for cultivation.

Terraces are an ancient way of preventing soil erosion and flooding. These terraces in Peru were made by the Incas hundreds of years ago.

Flood facts

These are some of the structural methods used to control flooding – and some of the problems that they bring.

- Dams are built high up on a river's course, to stop heavy mountain rains and snow meltwater from reaching the floodplain. Dams have spillways running from them, to stop them from overflowing. A spillway can be either a special channel or a part of the dam wall controlled by a floodgate.

- Dykes can drain water away from coastal and floodplain marshland so that it does not flood so easily – or they can act as a river overflow in times of flood. They need to be cleared regularly though.

- Embankments called **levees** can be raised on either side of the channel, although this cuts off water supplies to shallow-water habitats on the river's edge. **Sediment** washed down from the upper reaches of the river is concentrated on the narrowed river bed rather than spilling out onto the floodplain, and can clog the river if not looked after.

- Defensive walls made of concrete can be built to protect settlements along both coasts and rivers. They are also put up on the beach itself to stop **storm surges** eroding the cliffs. They have to be rebuilt or strengthened every 30 years to make sure they still offer protection.

- Pumping up groundwater during the dry season has been suggested as a partial solution to the problems of Bangladesh. It would lower the water table and leave room below ground for extra water during a flood. The water could be used for irrigating crops during the dry season.

- Re-planting programmes have been put into place in many areas, where **deforestation** has left vast areas of bare land over which floodwaters can easily flow, eroding soil which should act as a natural sponge.

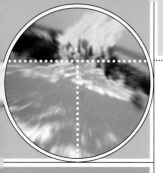

Striking a balance

Building flood prevention structures along a river channel can make flooding worse in other areas. Flood prevention methods can also spoil the environment. The problem is one of great concern in Bangladesh. Many ideas for improving river flood controls in Bangladesh have been suggested in the Flood Action Plan (see page 8) but the **floodplain** dwellers are worried. These measures could stop the beneficial effects of the **borsha** – the normal **monsoon** floods – and they will not help much in the **bonna** – the devastating floods. Flood control methods have not been without their problems in other parts of the world, either.

This flowering meadow along a **meandering** river shows how important the floodplain is for wildlife. People all over the world are realizing what they lose every time a river is straightened or restricted.

For and against

The Aswan High Dam in Egypt was completed in 1971 to control the annual flooding of the Nile. The dam lets farmers have more than one harvest each year, by storing water in the massive reservoir and releasing it more regularly. Irrigation projects have channelled the waters over a much wider area than the natural floods allowed, but the system is already causing problems of salination – too much salt in the soil. Crop yields are lower, too, because the fertile red soils that used to get washed down in the natural flood are now stuck behind the dam wall. Expensive artificial fertilizers have to be used, leaving too many **nitrates** in the soil.

Nature's sponges

Over the last hundred years about half of all the world's natural swamps, peat bogs and marshes have been drained. This has allowed more land to be used for agriculture and building, but it has also greatly increased the chance of **flash floods**, especially where dykes and ditches have not been properly maintained.

Not only do wetlands soak up a lot of water over a widespread area, but they also absorb chemicals such as nitrates. Without the wetlands, the nitrates drain freely into rivers. Vast areas of wetland habitat which are magnets for many species of birds, animals and plants have been destroyed.

In places the Rhine has been straightened, with tall concrete **levees** built along the banks. These measures certainly create efficient shipping channels but they also destroy shallow-water wildlife.

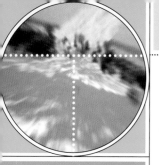

Nature rules, okay?

The flood of '93

Waters from over a quarter of the United States drain into the Mississippi and Missouri rivers, which flow onto a vast **floodplain** to the south and east. It is an area constantly troubled by flooding and many measures have been taken over more than a hundred years to stem the flow. Added to this, the parts of the Mississippi's course were straightened and deepened so that heavy shipping could transport goods from industrial areas along the banks of the floodplain.

Artificial flood protection methods actually contributed to the devastating floods of 1993 – the worst in over 150 years. Over 3000 kilometres (about 1900 miles) of concrete and earth **levees** had been built along the Mississippi, forcing the river into an ever-tighter, more restricted course. The deluge of rain was too much for the levees to hold and they burst their banks. Fifty people died and 93 000 square kilometres (36 000 square miles) of land were submerged, causing damage costing £6 billion (US$9.6 billion).

In the United States, the Heritage Conservation and Recreation Service has helped local governments to buy areas of floodplain around cities and towns. These are turned into conservation areas, which has stopped 15 000 hectares (37 000 acres) of land being built on.

Nowhere to flow

Building on fields of the floodplain and on wetlands creates areas of water-resistant concrete and tar. Overflowing waters from nearby rivers can no longer soak into the soil.

On 27 April 1999 in Birmingham, Britain's second largest city, the River Wray burst its banks for the second time in seven months. The flood was too fast for local residents to protect their houses with sandbags or rescue their belongings. The Environment Agency has now admitted what local residents had suspected for a long time – that nearby building programmes had covered fields that had previously soaked up floodwaters. The local council is now making £300 000 (US$480 000) available for a flood protection scheme along the Wray.

London is getting water-logged. The sheer weight of buildings is helping the water table to rise, increasing the threat of flooding. If a very high incoming tide from the coast coincides with heavy rainfall, then disaster beckons. It is hoped that the Thames Barrier, built to control floodwaters, will prevent this.

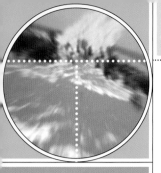

Flood aid

Coping with flood disaster

In the developing world, flood disaster can soon cause famine and disease. Crops are destroyed and water supplies are **contaminated**. It is these two problems that governments and aid agencies try to solve first, much as they do in drought disaster zones. They need food aid, **immunization** against disease, supplies of fresh water for drinking and cooking, and provision for sanitation and waste disposal.

It seems strange that emergency fresh water supplies are needed when there is so much water around but, even in rich countries, serious flooding causes sewage systems to overflow, mixing with fresh water both above and below the ground. Eventually the contaminated water finds its way into fresh water reservoirs which supply drinking water to homes. Often the water supply itself breaks down – there is no electricity to pump fresh water through pipes.

Paying the price

Between 1988 and 1989 Bangladesh spent about half of its annual development budget on repairing flood damage. Many developing countries have to take out money loans from foreign countries to pay for **infrastructures** such as bridges. In the Colombian floods of 1998, many bridges and roads were destroyed but the government still has to pay off the original loan for building them in the first place. As well as this, they now have to find more money to repair or rebuild these broken transport and communications systems.

In 1993, in the historic town of Saint Genevieve in the United States, the National Guard, the emergency services and 10 000 civilians worked to prevent a flood. But they lost the battle. This is the sewage plant, submerged by the floodwaters.

Flood facts

These are some of the most dangerous diseases that follow flood disaster. They can all be fatal. Added to these, most flood victims suffer from shock, exposure to the cold and stress.

- Typhoid is a bacterial infection causing **ulcers** on the intestines, high fever and identified by red spots on the skin.

- Cholera is a bacterial infection carried in food or water; it causes vomiting and diarrhoea.

- Yellow fever is caused by a virus transmitted, or carried, by mosquitoes. These insects hatch out in their billions after flooding in South America and Africa. It causes kidney infection and internal bleeding.

- Malaria is caused by a **parasite** transmitted by mosquitoes, bringing a very high fever. It weakens the body so that other diseases easily take hold.

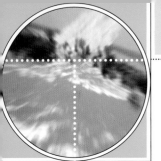

Underwater

Whenever flood swamps the land, swells the river or crushes the coast, everything underneath it changes. The lives of plants and animals are completely disrupted. But as the pictures show, floods produce both winners and losers in the natural world.

Covering the coast

Storm surges cover beaches, pushing sand and rock further inland and creating huge dunes. They smother the strong grasses and bushes that root themselves into the sand. The current underneath the swell is very strong and smashes coastal corals. As the wave retreats, the current digs into the sand, gravel and pebbles underneath, dragging them backwards. This disturbance is devastating for life in a coastal habitat, which may consist of rocks and exposed sands, and shallow waters. Here, many varieties of shellfish, worm, sponge and algae live.

Flooding from melting snow and avalanches in mountain areas can kill all the major vegetation, clearing areas for flowers, like these avalanche lilies.

This floodplain is in The Kimberley in Western Australia. The wide, slow **meanders** support life which is easily devastated by flash floods.

The raging river

Plants and animals living in the river on a **floodplain** are designed for life in quiet waters. Larger mammals make their homes in riverbank holes which can be swamped by floodwaters. Floating plants, like duckweed, or those with leaves that grow like balloons and float on the surface suffer badly in **flash floods**. They get tossed around and washed onto dry land where they cannot survive. So, too, do the creatures attached to them – among them dragonfly larvae and water beetles. Reeds, rushes and cat-tails are rooted into the river bed, and become battered by strong currents in flash floods.

On the floodplain itself, waterlogging loosens the soil around tree roots, weakening their hold. Smaller plants rot under water. Algae begin to grow on the **stagnant** water and the gases they produce help the plants to decompose, leaving fertile humus on the land once the floods recede. Mudflows that cover topsoil – a loose, airy mixture of humus and soils – stifle plant and animal life beneath, stopping essential gases from reaching them.

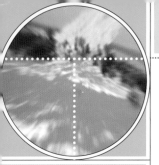

Surviving the flood

Some creatures are built for flood survival. On the coast the common limpet – a shellfish – clings tightly to the rocks and even digs out a small hole for itself. Plants and creatures that live in the steep torrents of water high up in a river's course have adapted to the raging river waters. Water moss clings to rocks by roots that grow in line with the current so they are less likely to be ripped from the rock by the flow. The larvae – or young – of some water insects are streamlined, again so that they move with the flow. But other creatures have adapted ways of escaping raging and rising waters rather than trying to survive them.

Some creatures have evolved to live out of the way of floods. Mammals such as the uakari monkey of the Amazon rainforest have made their homes in the treetops above the swampland, which can easily flood.

Slowly rising waters

Brazil's Amazon rainforest has some of the biggest floods every year, but we hear very little about them because they are predictable for both people and animals, who have time to prepare for them and adapt to them. The rainforest people build houserafts that are tethered to the riverbanks by ropes. They also build rafts for cattle and other livestock. The forest itself is flooded, allowing fishes and even dolphins to swim among the submerged tree trunks.

Fire ants actually use the floods to travel and spread across the forest. Huge colonies respond to the flooding by make a living raft. The worker ants link their legs together and the others stand on them. The whole 'vessel' then floats along the flooded river until it settles near a dry bank. Then, the queen and other important ants step over their raft of workers to the safety of dry land, where a new nest is built.

Sudden floods

On the Barrier Islands off the coast of Virginia in the United States, seabirds have no **predators** such as raccoons, so they nest happily on the sands. Loggerhead turtles bury their eggs in them, too – usually higher up than the birds, away from the water. But the sands are very lowlying and can get swamped by a **storm surge**, which crashes onto the shore in a wall of water 4 metres (12 feet) high. Young turtles and chicks drown, but the sand gets formed into different shapes further up the beach, giving new breeding grounds for birds and turtles alike.

Plants that have evolved to cope with relentlessly dry weather conditions just cannot adapt to the rare experience of floodwater. These olive trees would be unable to absorb the necessary nutrients in a flood and would die and rot away.

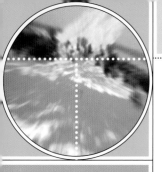

Floods in history

Proving the past

People all over the world have their flood disaster myths, legends and religious stories. Many were based on ancient truths that are now difficult but not impossible to prove.

Using the tools described in the Flood facts box opposite, and others, scientists have worked out that about 5000 years ago the Black Sea broke through a strip of land between what is now Turkey and the Balkan peninsula, flooding an area now known as the Sea of Marmara. It also created a narrow strait connecting the two seas, called the Bosporus.

A flood of floods

We are probably not talking about just one flood in the Sea of Marmara. The fact is that the whole world was going through incredible climatic change from about 10 000 BCE. Ice caps were slipping, ice sheets were melting, the sea was rising and coasts and islands were submerging beneath the waves.

It will take a long time to piece together a picture of the world before the great floods, caused by the masses of melting ice, swept away peoples and places. In caves that now lie under the sea there is evidence of stalactites and stalagmites – long, hard columns of calcium carbonate rock. These were made when rain falling on limestone pavements lying high on the Earth's surface, dripped through onto the hollow caves' floors and ceilings. These are evidence of a dry world of long ago. Exactly how and why such turbulent and dramatic change took place is harder to find out.

Fourteen thousand years ago a natural dam of ice broke and a waterfall 8 kilometres (5 miles) wide crashed through Montana in the United States, making a huge lake that carved out a channel 100 times bigger than the River Amazon.

Flood facts

These are two ways of finding out about floods of the past.

- **Dendrochronology** is the study of tree rings. Each ring shows a year's growth. In a dry year the ring will be thin, while in a wet year it will be wider. In the event of a flood, the cells in the ring appear to be damaged. Dendrochronology also helps to date floods.

- Dating flood deposits involves the study of soils, **silt**, gravel and boulders that are transported onto the **floodplain** during a flood. Their thickness and spread can show the severity of a flood, but dating them is a problem unless fragments of plants can be found in them. If they can, then a process called **radio-carbon dating** can show when the deposits were laid down, and therefore when the flood occurred.

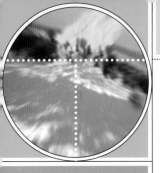

Fatal floods

It is difficult to know whether the deaths in these top ten flood disasters were caused directly by drowning, mudslides, disease or famine due to ruined crops. Whatever the cause it is clear that flooding is one of the most lethal and terrifying natural disasters.

Top ten flood disasters

Year	Place	No. of deaths (approximately)
1931	Huang Ho, China	4 000 000
1887	Honan, China	900 000
1970	Bangladesh	500 000
1642	China	300 000
1911	Yangtze, China	100 000
1920	China	100 000
1786	Japan	30 000
1999	Venezuela	30 000
1828	Japan	10 000
1951	Manchuria, China	5 000

Dangerous driving

Advanced flood prediction and warning systems prevent hundreds of deaths – but not all. Most deaths that do occur now are caused by motorists driving through low floodwaters which suddenly turn into **flash floods**. It takes only 15 centimetres (6 inches) of water to stop a car in its tracks – after that, the motorist and passengers should abandon the car and make a run for it. But not all do – and not all can.

In the south-west of the United States in spring, 7.5–10 centimetres (about 3–4 inches) of rain can fall in just one hour. In lowlying areas where streams and rivers flow, this means that waters can rise 60 centimetres (2 feet) in just two to three minutes. Each rising 30 centimetres (1 foot) of water puts 1100 kilograms (500 pounds) of pressure against the car. This is enough to stop passengers from opening the doors and escaping.

Flood facts

- The heaviest rainforest rain occurs in Liberia in West Africa. Here, huge raindrops batter the canopy at a rate of 40 centimetres (about 16 inches) of rainfall per hour.

- In 1952, the floods in Lynmouth, on the west coast of England were so fast and furious that huge boulders were swept downriver smashing bridges and blocking the channel.

- In 1950 in the United States, about 10 million people lived in the way of floods. By 1970 this had reached 20 million. Now, over 31 million people are in danger.

- In 1998, along the three main rivers of south-west Pakistan, mud nearly 2 metres (6.5 feet) high swept 500 kilometres (311 miles) downstream, smothering and destroying all the settlements in its way.

In Iceland, volcanoes can melt glaciers. In November 1996, glacial floodwater caused damage costing £2 million (US $3.2 million). The water carried tonnes of black volcanic sand which smothered pastures and crops.

Glossary

ALERT Automated Local Evaluation in Real Time – the flood alert system of the United States

altitude height above sea-level

bonna heavy, destructive flooding that sometimes occurs in Bangladesh

borsha normal, beneficial flooding that occurs every year in Bangladesh

carbon gases gases given off when fossil fuels like coal and oil are burned

catchment area the area from which all surface and underground water runs into a single main river

contaminate to poison with harmful bacteria or chemicals

contour ploughing ploughing fields in curves so that water does not run straight down the furrows, causing soil erosion

cyclone tropical storm (see 'hurricane' below)

deforestation cutting down forest

delta the mouth of the river – where the river meets the sea

dendrochronology the study of tree rings to find out climatic changes

discharge the amount of water passing a particular point after rainfall has occurred

drainage basin the land around a main river system, including all the streams and all the water that soaks into the soil

El Niño a weather phenomenon in which the direction of prevailing winds is reversed and ocean currents warm up causing violent changes in weather

estuary very lowlying, wide, wet area where the river meets the sea

evacuate to move to safety

evaporate/evaporation when a liquid is turned into a gas

evapotranspiration the loss of water by evaporation or by transpiration through plant leaves

flash flood sudden, very high floodwaters, often caused by very heavy or prolonged rainfall

floodplain the low flat area of land around where the river widens

fossil fuels fuels such as coal and gas

global warming the warming of the Earth's climate

greenhouse effect layers of gases in the atmosphere reflect back the Sun's heat energy radiating from the Earth

hazard mapping/maps mapping areas most likely to suffer from disaster

high pressure an area of cool, dry descending air

hurricane a fierce, whirling wind that blows in an inward spiral – it brings rainstorms and flooding (also called a tropical cyclone or a typhoon)

hydrograph measures the amount of water passing a certain point in a streamflow after rainfall has occurred

immunization protection against diseases, usually given as injections

impermeable soil and rock that does not absorb water easily

infrastructures basic facilities in a community, such as roads, railways, telephones, electricity and water supplies

inundate to completely swamp

irrigate artificially water

lag-time the time it takes for all rainfall from a particular downpour to reach a water channel

La Niña the reversal of the action on the climate of the El Niño effect

levees embankments

loess a fine yellow, powdery soil, found in thick layers in northern China, easily worn away by water

low pressure   an area of warm, moist rising air causes low air pressure

meandering   when a river winds and loops along a floodplain

monsoon   means 'seasonal' and marks the change in winds that occurs twice-yearly in south-east Asia, bringing torrential rain and flooding in summer

nitrate   a chemical that makes the soil more fertile, but too much is harmful

North Atlantic Oscillation (NAO)   a change in air pressure and wind above the Atlantic, affecting weather in western Europe and North Africa

ozone   a thin layer of protective gas high up above the Earth's surface

paddy fields   rice-growing fields that are flooded during the growing season

parasite   a creature that lives on or inside another creature

percolate   when water seeps through rock or soil

permeable   soil and rock that absorbs water easily

phosphate   a chemical that makes the soil more fertile

precipitation   the fall of rain, sleet, snow, hail or mist

predator   a creature that hunts other animals in order to kill them for food

radiate/radiation   energy given out in rays, like light or heat from the Sun

radio-carbon dating   used to find out how old something is by measuring the amount of radioactive carbon left in plant matter such as wood

run-off   water running along and over the ground

saturated   when something, eg: soil, cannot absorb any more water

sediment   fine soils deposited by rivers and streams

silt   very fine soil eroded by river water and deposited near the river's mouth

soil erosion   wearing away of topsoils, which get washed away by floodsd

spring tide   when the Moon and the Sun are set in a straight line so that their gravity pulls together strongly on the Earth, making high tides even higher

stagnant   still water that has very little oxygen in it, making it poisonous

storm surge   a band of very low air pressure over the ocean sucks up the sea causing a wall of water to crash ashore

stratosphere   the layer of atmosphere lying between 10 and 50 kilometres above the Earth's surface

throughflow   the amount of water soaking or running through the ground and into a stream, river or lake

tidal bore   a high wave caused by an incoming tide squeezing up a narrow estuary, that travels up the river as a wall of water often a metre or more high

tropics   the areas immediately above and below the equator, lying about 23 degrees north or south of it

tropopause   the boundary between the troposphere and statosphere in the atmosphere

troposphere   the layer of atmosphere closest to the Earth's surface

typhoon   see 'hurricane' above

ulcer   an open wound – often used to describe a hole in the stomach lining

ultra-violet rays   light outside the range of visible wavelengths, which comes from the Sun

water cycle   the way in which water is continually recycled in different forms – as water, hail, ice, snow or vapour (gas)

water vapour   water in its gaseous state – it has been heated until the molecules expand and change into a gas

watershed   high ground that divides one river catchment area from another

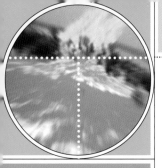

Index